# HAPAX

 # HAPAX

P O E M S

A. E. Stallings

**TRIQUARTERLY BOOKS**
*Northwestern University Press*
*Evanston, Illinois*

TriQuarterly Books
Northwestern University Press
www.nupress.northwestern.edu

Copyright © 2006 by A. E. Stallings. Published 2006 by
TriQuarterly Books/Northwestern University Press.
All rights reserved.

Printed in the United States of America

10   9   8   7

ISBN-13: 978-0-8101-5170-3 (cloth)
ISBN-10: 0-8101-5170-7 (cloth)
ISBN-13: 978-0-8101-5171-0 (paper)
ISBN-10: 0-8101-5171-5 (paper)

Library of Congress Cataloging-in-Publication data are
available from the Library of Congress.

⊗ The paper used in this publication meets the
minimum requirements of the American National
Standard for Information Sciences—Permanence of
Paper for Printed Library Materials, ANSI Z39.48-1992.

*for John*

## HAPAX / ΑΠΑΞ

ἅπαξ: once, once only, once for all

First citation:

Σχέτλιοι, οἳ ζώοντες ὑπήλθετε δῶμ' Ἀΐδαο,
δισθανέες, ὅτε τ' ἄλλοι ἅπαξ θνήσκουσ' ἄνθρωποι.

Foolhardy ones! You went alive down to the hall of Hades,
Mortals twice over, when other men die only once.
—*Odyssey*, 12:21–22

hapax: [by shortening] hapax legomenon, a word or form
evidenced by a single citation; a word or form occurring
once and only once in a document or corpus

# CONTENTS

# VI

# HAPAX

 I

# Aftershocks

We are not in the same place after all.
The only evidence of the disaster,
Mapping out across the bedroom wall,
Tiny cracks still fissuring the plaster—
A new cartography for us to master,
In whose legend we read where we are bound:
Terra infirma, a stranger land, and vaster.
Or have we always stood on shaky ground?
The moment keeps on happening: a sound.
The floor beneath us swings, a pendulum
That clocks the heart, the heart so tightly wound,
We fall mute, as when two lovers come
To the brink of the apology, and halt,
Each standing on the wrong side of the fault.

# The Dollhouse

There in the attic of forgotten shapes
(Old coats in plastic, hatboxes, fur capes
Amongst the smells of mothballs and cigars),
I saw the dollhouse of our early years,
With which my mother and my aunt had played,
And later where my sister and I made
The towering grown-up hours to smile and pass:
The little beds, the tinfoil looking glass,
Bookcases stamped in ink upon the walls,
Mismatched chairs where sat the jointed dolls,
The clock whose face, no larger than a dime,
Had, for all these years, kept the same time.
I remembered how we set the resin food
Atop a table of stained balsa wood,
The shiny turkey hollow to the tap,
The cherry pie baked in a bottle cap.
Now it is time to go to sleep, we spoke,
Parroting the talk of older folk,
And laid the dolls out fully clothed in bed
After their teeth were brushed, and prayers were said,
And flipped the switch on the low-wattage sun.

But in the night we'd have something break in,
Kidnap the baby or purloin the pie—
A tiger, maybe, or a passerby—
Just to make something happen, to move the story.
The dolls awoke, alarmed, took inventory.
If we made something happen every day,
Or night, it was the game we knew to play,
Not realizing then how lives accrue,
With interest, the smallest things we do.

# Lovejoy Street

The house where we were happy,
Perhaps it's standing still
On the wrong side of the railroad tracks
Half-way down the hill.

Perhaps new people live there
Who think the street name quaint,
And watch the dogwood petals shiver
Down like flakes of paint.

Perhaps they hold each other
When the train goes railing by,
Shaking up the windowpanes
And dressing down the sky.

And perhaps it strikes them rich
When spring is making shift,
To find the bank in blooming pink
Where we had planted thrift.

Perhaps they reap our roses
In an antique jelly jar.
And maybe they are happy there,
And do not know they are.

# The Village in the Lake

*Lake Lanier*


It is not a natural lake,
It was made for pleasure's sake:
For speedboaters, and those who swish
On water skis. It's stocked with fish.
Its waters are not clear, but brown.
Every summer, children drown,
Or teenagers, addled with beer
And showing off, along a pier,
Push each other in, or dive,
And are not seen again alive.
Even sober grown-ups taught
In scuba diving can get caught
In a submerged tree or vine,
Or tangled in old fishing line.

There are those who tell me down
At the bottom is a town,
Flooded years and years ago:
Houses, and a Texaco.
Somewhere a cemetery lies.
How could it be otherwise?
Yet I wonder of those dead
(All that water overhead),
Who were buried underground:

Can ghosts swim? Or are they drowned,
Sinking slowly in the mud,
While in the treetops fishes scud,
And through the murky heavens floats
The shadow of the pleasure boats?

# Sine Qua Non

Your absence, father, is nothing. It is naught—
The factor by which nothing will multiply,
The gap of a dropped stitch, the needle's eye
Weeping its black thread. It is the spot
Blindly spreading behind the looking glass.
It is the startled silences that come
When the refrigerator stops its hum,
And crickets pause to let the winter pass.

Your absence, father, is nothing—for it is
Omega's long last O, memory's elision,
The fraction of impossible division,
The element I move through, emptiness,
The void stars hang in, the interstice of lace,
The zero that still holds the sum in place.

# Last Will

What he *really* wanted, she confesses,
Was to be funnelled into shells and shot
Across a dove-field. Only, she could not—

The kick of shotguns knocks her over. Well,
I say, he'd understand. It doesn't matter
What becomes of atoms, how they scatter.

The priest reads the committal, something short.
We drop the little velvet pouch of dust
Down a cylindrical hole bored in the clay—

And one by one, the doves descend, ash-gray,
Softly as cinders on the parking lot,
And silence sounds its deafening report.

# Arrowhead Hunting

The land is full of what was lost. What's hidden
Rises to the surface after rain
In new-ploughed fields, and fields stubbled again:
The clay shards, foot and lip, that heaped the midden,

And here and there a blade or flakes of blade,
A patient art, knapped from a core of flint,
Most broken, few as coins new from the mint,
Perfect, shot through time as through a glade.

You cannot help but think how they were lost:
The quarry, fletched shaft in its flank, the blood
Whose trail soon vanished in the antlered wood,
Not just the meat, but what the weapon cost—

O hapless hunter, though your aim was true—
The spooked hart, wounded, fleeting in its fear—
And the sharpness honed with longing, year by year
Buried deeper, found someday, but not by you.

# *Ubi Sunt* Lament for the Eccentric Museums
## of My Childhood

Orphaned oddments crammed
in university base-
ments, in corridors

of state capitols,
identified by jaundiced
index cards, I think

about you now—where
have the curators of new
collections stashed you?—

a clutch of geodes
cracked like dragon eggs in mid-
metamorphosis,

coins trite from dead hands,
the two-headed calf floating
in amniotics

of formaldehyde.
Where is Doc Holiday's old
dentist chair? the lone

token mummy, sans
sarcophagus, all unrav-
elling bandages?

(On dares, we looked up
his double-barrelled nose at
cocked eternity.)

Is he under wraps
now, x-rayed, with a puffed-up
provenance, rewound,

educational?
Curators, where are the lost
curiosities,

stranded at random
on Time's littered littoral?
Why, we used to muse,

did this thing, not that,
survive its gone moment—how
are they filed away?

# Thyme

I have some of it still,
We gathered on the hill,
In an empty glass, the bunch of wild thyme,

Faded now, and dried,
But in which yet abide
Some purple, a smell of summer in its prime,

When we stopped the car
Bought honey in a jar
At a roadside stand. It makes me think about

The theft of bloom, the sting,
A swiftness on the wing,
Things that sweetness cannot be without.

**II**

# Implements from the "Tomb of the Poet"

*Piraeus Archaeological Museum*

On the journey to the mundane afterlife,
You travel equipped to carry on your trade:
A bronze, small-toothed saw to make repairs,
The stylus and the inkpot and the scraper,
Wax tablets bound into a little book.

Here is the tortoise shell for the kithara,
Bored through with holes for strings, natural sound box.
Here is the harp's wood triangle, all empty—
The sheep gut having long since de-composed
Into a pure Pythagorean music.

The beeswax, frangible with centuries,
Has puzzled all your lyrics into silence.
I think you were a poet of perfection
Who fled still weighing one word with another,
Since wax forgives and warms beneath revision.

# Visiting the Grave of Rupert Brooke

*Island of Skyros, Greece*


Rupert, this was where, I'm sure you knew,
The sea nymph Thetis took Achilles to,
And hid him, with his smooth cheek and gold curls,
Among the royal retinue of girls,
As any mother might, to save her son,
From war and death, by arrow or the gun.
Odysseus, recruiting, in disguise,
Set out for sale a range of merchandise,
Stuffs no princess easily resists—
Fine brocades, and bangles for the wrists,
All manner of adornments, silver, gold,
And set a blade among them, brazen, cold—
A simple trap that might catch any boy.
But only old men made it home from Troy.

# The Charioteer

*Delphi Museum*

Lips apart, dry eyes steady,
He stands forever at the ready,

Fingers open, sensitive
To the horses' take and give

(Although no single steed remains
At the end of tangled reins).

It is as if we are not here—
The way the patient charioteer

Looks beyond us, into space,
For some sign to begin the race.

He has stared down centuries.
No wave from us, no sudden breeze,

Will trick him now to a false start.
He has learned the racer's art

To stand watchful at the gate,
Empty out the mind, and wait.

As long as it is in our power
We gaze—maybe for half an hour—

Before we turn from him to go.
Outside, the hills begin to glow,

Burnished by a brazen sun
Whose course now is almost run.

We shiver, and around us feel
Vanished horses plunge and wheel.

# Asphodel

*after the words of Penny Turner, Nymphaion, Greece*

Our guide turned in her saddle, broke the spell:
"You ride now through a field of asphodel,
The flower native to the plains of hell.

Across just such a field the pale shade came
Of proud Achilles, who had preferred a name
And short life to a long life without fame,

And summoned by Odysseus he gave
This wisdom, 'Better by far to be a slave
Among the living, than great among the grave.'

I used to wonder, how did such a bloom
Become associated with the tomb?
Then one evening, walking through the gloom,

I noticed a strange fragrance. It was sweet,
Like honey—but with hints of rotting meat.
An army of them bristled at my feet."

# An Ancient Dog Grave, Unearthed During Construction of the Athens Metro

It is not the curled-up bones, nor even the grave
That stops me, but the blue beads on the collar
(Whose leather has long gone the way of hides)—
The ones to ward off evil. A careful master
Even now protects a favorite, just so.
But what evil could she suffer after death?
I picture the loyal companion, bereaved of her master,
Trotting the long, dark way that slopes to the river,
Nearly trampled by all the nations marching down,
One war after another, flood or famine,
Her paws sucked by the thick, caliginous mud,
Deep as her dewclaws, near the riverbank.
In the press for the ferry, who will lift her into the boat?
Will she cower under the pier and be forgotten,
Forever howling and whimpering, tail tucked under?
What stranger pays her passage? Perhaps she swims,
Dog-paddling the current of oblivion.
A shake as she scrambles ashore sets the beads jingling.
And then, that last, tense moment—touching noses
Once, twice, three times, with unleashed Cerberus.

# Actaeon

The hounds, you know them all by name.
You fostered them from purblind whelps
At their dam's teats, and you have come
To know the music of their yelps—

High-strung Anthee, the brindled bitch,
The bluetick-coated Philomel,
And freckled Chloë, who would fetch
A pretty price if you would sell—

All fleet of foot, and swift to scent,
Inexorable once on the track,
Like angry words you might have meant,
But do not mean, and can't take back.

There was a time when you would brag
How they would bay and rend apart
The hopeless belling from a stag.
You falter now for the foundered hart.

Desires you nursed of a winter night—
Did you know then why you bred them—
Whose needling milk teeth used to bite
The master's hand that leashed and fed them?

# The Modern Greek for "Nightmare"
## Is *Ephialtes*

I think, what brought you to this pass?
Heroes lie thick, anonymous,

Blurred with honorable mention
In mass graves of fine intention,

And yet even now dreams yield
On their unequal battlefield

Betrayal's still familiar face,
The name that nothing can erase,

Not even final victory.
Sleep has no sense of history:

Even now I lose the day,
Always look the other way,

While old treachery awaits
The heart's warm springs, its hot gates.

# Dead Language Lesson

They lift their half-closed eyes out of the grammar.

What is the object of love? *You,*
*Singular.* The subject? *I.*

Aeneas has nothing to say for himself.
Even the boys confess that he
Didn't intend to come back, the girls
Already know the tale by heart.

They wheedle me for tangents, for
Anything not in a book,
Even though it's all from books:
The many-wiled Penelope,
Orpheus struck dumb with hindsight.

I confiscate a note in which
The author writes, "who do you love?"—
An agony past all correction.

I think, as they wait for the bell,
Blessed are the young for whom
All languages are dead: the girl
Who twines her golden hair, like Circe,
Turning glib boys into swine.

# First Love: A Quiz

He came up to me:

    a. in his souped-up Camaro

    b. to talk to my skinny best friend

    c. and bumped my glass of wine so I wore the ferrous stain on my sleeve

    d. from the ground, in a lead chariot drawn by a team of stallions black as crude oil and breathing sulfur; at his heart, he sported a tiny golden arrow

He offered me:

    a. a ride

    b. dinner and a movie, with a wink at the cliché

    c. an excuse not to go back alone to the apartment with its sink of dirty knives

    d. a narcissus with a hundred dazzling petals that breathed a sweetness as cloying as decay

I went with him because:

    a. even his friends told me to beware

    b. I had nothing to lose except my virginity

    c. he placed his hand in the small of my back and I felt the tread of honeybees

    d. he was my uncle, the one who lived in the half-finished basement, and he took me by the hair

The place he took me to:

    a. was dark as my shut eyes

    b. and where I ate bitter seed and became ripe

    c. and from which my mother would never take me wholly back, though she wept and walked the earth and made the bearded ears of barley wither on their stalks and the blasted flowers drop from their sepals

    d. is called by some men hell and others love

    e. all of the above

# Mint

*Menthe*


I was at a loss,
Growing up wild
Among the dross and rust
Of nowhere, when he smiled—

King of the appetites,
King of shade and dust.
I met him at the cross-
Roads of love and lust.

When pale Jealousy yanked
My heart out by the roots,
She trod it into the ground
With her flint-soled boots;

But trampled into earth
I did not quit the place,
I shed my heart's blood
As a kind of grace.

Oh, pungent and sweet
The juices that I bleed!
The heart springs afresh
As a rank weed.

Now I mask and flavor
Decay beneath the breath,
Consecrated ever
To the King of Death.

# Nettles

March: pinked leaflets sprout
from nooks and chinks, peeking out
like shy faith from doubt,

like spring from winter.
Surprising still, how tender
they start, and render,

with pale green pardons,
vacant lots, sudden gardens,
till summer hardens

his hot argument,
and gentleness is spent, spent,
nor will dust relent.

Then the nettles wedged
by pots on the window ledge
lash out like a grudge

at blind blunders—herb,
like hate or love, barb by barb,
grown from noun to verb.

# Flying Colors: Flags of Convenience

※

In the cheek flies the blood's red semaphore.
Has it been struck? Or is it signing shame,
Or love—one of whose corners dragged the ground?
The proper way to dispose of it is burning.

※

Standards of distance—cerulean, ultramarine,
Indigo. Point where all perspectives taper—
The mountain ridge like torn construction paper.
The voice bending, "My baby done gone and left me."

※

Green snaps to attention in the trees,
Grass parading Independence Day.
But oh, it is deciduous, deciduous.
False summer is pledging his allegiance.

※

Dawn rises blank, hungover. Laundry pinned
Out on the front line waves its wan despair—
*I give up*—the morning after the night
Of drunken fighting. Three sheets to the wind.

# "To Speke of Wo That Is in Mariage"

"It is a choreography as neat
As two folding up a laundered sheet,
The way we dance around what we would say:
Approach, meet, touch, then slowly back away.

To sweep is to know what gathers there
Beneath the bed: sloughed cells, lost strands of hair.
To wash clothes well is to take certain pains:
The sad and sordid stories of the stains.

Although my anger may be slow to boil,
I have the smoking point of olive oil.
Every time I wield a knife, I cry.
He has become the onion of my eye.

I dwell upon, it's true. He will not linger.
When I grow cold, the ring slips from my finger."

# Purgatory

Laundry drops into the trees
From overlooking balconies
And hangs, mid-plummet, in mid-air—

T-shirts, socks, and underwear—
Gone papery and shapeless, stiff,
Bleached and ragged. It's as if

These were the husks of soiled souls,
Empty now, and full of holes,
Flensed from bodies, hung between

Two lives, for winds to lick them clean,
So that they could be worn afresh,
Pure as any newborn flesh.

But these will never rise or fall,
Caught in the middle. This is all:
Exposure to the elements,

The sun, the wind. The raw suspense.

# Fragment

The glass does not break because it is glass,
Said the philosopher. The glass could stay
Unbroken forever, shoved back in a dark closet,
Slowly weeping itself, a colorless liquid.
The glass breaks because somebody drops it
From a height—a grip stunned open by bad news
Or laughter. A giddy sweep of grand gesture
Or fluttering nerves might knock it off the table—
Or perhaps wine emptied from it, into the blood,
Has numbed the fingers. It breaks because it falls
Into the arms of the earth—that grave attraction.
It breaks because it meets the floor's surface,
Which is solid and does not give. It breaks because
It is dropped, and falls hard, because it hits
Bottom, and because nobody catches it.

# Failure

You humble in. It's just as you remember:
The sallow walls, formica countertop,

The circular argument of time beneath
Fluorescent flickering: doubt, faith, and doubt.

She knows you've been to see the gilded girl
Who's always promising and walking out

With someone else. She knew that you'd return,
With nothing in your pockets but your fists.

Why do you resist? When will you learn
That this is what your weary dreams are of—

Succumbing to Her unconditional love?

# Noir

Late at night,
One of us sometimes has said,
Watching a movie in black and white,
Of the vivid figures quick upon the screen,
"Surely by now all of them are dead"—
The yapping, wire-haired terrier, of course—
And the patient horse
Soaked in an illusion of London rain,
The Scotland Yard inspector at the scene,
The extras—faces in the crowd, the sailors—
The bungling blackmailers,
The kidnapped girl's parents, reunited again
With their one and only joy, lisping in tones antique
As that style of pouting Cupid's bow
Or those plucked eyebrows, arched to the height of chic.

Ignorant of so many things we know,
How they seem innocent, and yet they too
Possess a knowledge that they cannot give,
The grainy screen a kind of sieve
That holds some things, but lets some things slip through

With the current's rush and swirl.
We wonder briefly only about the girl—
How old—seven, twelve—it isn't clear—
Perhaps she's still alive
Watching this somewhere at eighty-five,
The only one who knows, though we might guess,
What the kidnapper whispers in her ear,
Or the color of her dress.

# Alice, Grown-up, at the Cocktail Party

The bottle still says, "Drink me." I still feel
All knees and elbows in a room, half hope
To shut up tidy as a telescope.
The nonsense people talk! Oh to walk out
Through a little door, into the crepusculum
Of a private garden, the only person there
Save for the nodding idiocy of flowers.
The hours pass, a slow murder of Time.
Always the golden key sits out of reach.
Always people riddle me with questions
For which there are no answers; always the wrong
Words tumble out to fill the awkward breach,
Like half-remembered lyrics from a song.
I've lost the trick of dealing packs of lies
In spades, so that the trumped heart follows suit.
The bottle still says, "Drink me." One obeys.
If only I could forget things as they pass,
Amnesiac as the glaucous looking glass,
Or stop that sinking feeling I am falling.
Oh, to walk out the door, to where the moon
Hangs like a disembodied head's queer smile
In the branches of the trees, the curious while
Till the sun comes up and paints the roses red.

# Cassandra

If I may have failed to follow
Your instructions, Lord Apollo,
So all my harping lies unstrung,
I blame it on the human tongue.

Our speech ever was at odds
With the utterance of gods:
Tenses have no paradigm
For those translated out of time.

Perhaps mortals should rejoice
To conjugate in passive voice—
The alphabet to which I go
Is suffering, and ends in O.

Paraphrase can only worsen:
For you, there is no second person,
"I want" the same verb as "must be,"
"Love," construed as "yield to me,"

The homonym of "curse" and "give,"
No mood but the infinitive.

IV

# Clean Break

In a crenellated town, wearily bright,
They learned how a new language was construed,
And bathed all things in the subjunctive mood
    Like a dappled light.

Old enough to know they were too young,
They could foresee the end, which made them wise:
They promised nothing, and they told no lies,
    Not in their native tongue.

They parted well on the appointed day,
Out in the plaza, underneath the noon,
While that summer's iterative tune
    Pulsed from a café.

It ended cleanly as it had begun.
He rode facing the wrong way on the train.
Watching gold fields of sunflowers strain
    For hindsight of the sun,

He thought of their farewell—almost sublime,
How there were no regrets—they'd been too clever—
Not knowing yet that that kind of forever
    Happens all the time.

# Evil Eye

"Yes, it's on you," Kalliópe frowns,
Dribbling amber beads of olive oil
Down thick fingers into the water glass
Where they amass
In one big cyclops-blob, and do not scatter.

Something, it seems, always *is* the matter.
Vague pains, or clumsy accidents, a dim
Nimbus on my head, a personal cloud.
Perhaps she *is* endowed
With second sight. I'm lifted by a loss

As she thumbs my forehead with a cross;
Anointed, for a moment, I forget
The failed rehearsals of a mirth, and grief
Floods me like relief.
Yes, something's wrong, something she can *see*.

Even you glance differently at me
For half a second, though we do not believe
In village superstition. Still, we ask,
And she performs the task:
I always have it, and she always takes

It off of me (which gives her stomachaches).
And we are grateful, but do not offer thanks—
That would undo it somehow. We walk out
Like shadows of a doubt
Into the changed look of the afternoon.

# Apotropaic

Pity Evil his quaintness and old-fangled
Manners, his age, his nerves so raw that bells
And firecrackers leave him spooked and jangled.
Shy of onion, garlic, pungent smells,

His stomach thrown off by a pinch of salt,
He hankers for blandness like an invalid.
He stands on ceremony. He will halt
When not invited in. You can be rid

Of his presence by vulgarity—eschew
His curious eye by spitting, and offend
His queer aesthetics with the color blue.
Beauty attracts him. He's quick to befriend

The lucky, the talented, the heaven-sent—
At your service, if not your command—
Courtly, brought close by a compliment,
Bowing, with his black hat in his hand.

# Amateur Iconography: Resurrection

## *The Harrowing of Hell*

Jesus is back—he's harvesting the dead.
He's pulling them up out of the dirt like leeks—
By the scruff of the neck, by the wispy hair on the head,
Like bulbs in darkness sallowly starting to grow

From deep down in the earth where the lost things go—
Keys and locks, small change, old hinges, nails.
(That's why the living beseech the dead, who know
Where missing objects lie.) Jesus has a grip

On Adam by the left wrist—he will not slip—
And Eve, by her right. They're groggy and don't understand,
They died so long ago. With trembling lip,
Adam surveys the crowds of new people. And Eve

Looks up the emptiness of her limp left sleeve
For the hand that was unforgiven and is no more,
Ages since withered to dust, and starts to grieve
The sinister loss, recalling the heft in that hand

Of the flesh of the fruit, and the lightness at the core.

# Empty Icon Frame

*Glykophilousa, Virgin of Tenderness*


The preciousness was mortal: pigment and wood—
    Dissolved to dust, they leave behind
        Vacancies the mind
Fills in, imagining the faces good

And sorrowful: the mother's kiss, the child
    Oddly wizened, his grave gesture,
        His gaze nailed to the future,
His lips slightly curved as if they smiled.

We know the archetype, so we can see
    From outlines, the old attitudes,
        The chroma that eludes
Us now, expanse of lapis lazuli

Lavished only on her modest raiment,
    Those heaven-saturated blues,
        Costliest of hues—
Spending in itself a kind of payment—

And haloes gently brushed in powdered gold
    Ruddy and rich, which this carapace
        Of silver would replace
In time—every flowing lap and fold

Of garment, where his phantom small hand clings,
Hammered now in stiff relief
And gilded in gold leaf,
Glinting like armor—the metal renderings

Defining absence, as if its silhouette meant
That somehow soft flesh could be thirled
Forever to the world,
Or Love outlast its glittering revetment.

# Exile: Picture Postcards

### i. Athens, August

Even the days of the week have fled for the islands.
In the broken shadow of ruins, tourists huddle.
The citizens have vanished, melted away
In August's neutron bomb, its blinding silence.
A remnant of the faithful at the bus stop
Awaits the coming of the four-nineteen.
The pigeons mill through empty squares, at a loss.
No one heeds the prophecy of cicadas.

In dusty parks beneath the tattered palms,
Bareheaded statues cannot shade their eyes;
Stray dogs lap water from a leaking spigot.
As the sun reaches the height of absurdity,
A tree lets drop a single yellow leaf
To the pavement like a used bus ticket.

### ii. Mornings, I Walk Past the First Cemetery of Athens

Like a widow, every day the grey Dawn comes
To the Proto Nekrotapheío, and sweeps the crumbs
Of Night from tombstones, and the marble busts.

The stonecutter in his workshop contemplates,
Chisel in hand, the blank face of clean slates.
The waitress at the café mops and dusts.

A priest sits at his newspaper and tarries
Over the headlines and obituaries.

Soon, the mourners gather there to drain
The thick black liquid to the bitter grain.
At the Office of Endings, a hunched man taps his thumbs.

Four diggers play a hand of cards to kill
A little time; two withered florists fill
The old foam wreaths with new chrysanthemums.


*iii. Bouzouki*

After five years here, I understand
Most of the sung words, recognize the tune,
But there's an element I'll never get,

That isn't born in me. The way they play—
One manages to hold his cigarette
Between two fingers on his strumming hand,

Takes drags between his solos—and then soon
How something changes: a woman starts to sway
Around an absent center—ancient wrongs

Cherished. The cigarette gives up its ghost.
The music drives now. Someone makes a toast
As suddenly the melody arrives

At minor,
   Asia Minor,
      in whose songs

The hands of lovers always rhyme with knives.


*iv. The City*
 after C. P. Cavafy

You said, "I'll go to another land, I'll go to another sea.
I'll find another city. One that is better than this.
Here my every effort is sentenced to fruitlessness,
And here my heart's entombed, as if it were a cadaver.
How long will my mind loiter in this wasteland? For wherever
I turn my eyes here, whatever I look upon,
I see the black wreckage of my life, all the gone
Years I frittered away, destroyed, wasted utterly."

But you will find no other lands, no other seas discover.
This city will pursue you. The same streets, you will follow.
You will grow old among the neighborhoods that you know now.
Among the same houses, you will turn grey. Forever
You are coming to this city. Do not expect another.
For you there is no ship. There is no road for you.
For as you've wrecked your life in this small corner, so too
You have wrecked your life the whole world over.

# Minutes

Minutes swarm by, holding their dirty hands out,
Begging change, loose coins of your spare attention.
No one has the currency for them always;
        Most go unnoticed.

Some are selling packets of paper tissues,
Some sell thyme they found growing wild on hillsides,
Some will offer shreds of accordion music,
        Sad and nostalgic.

Some have only cards with implausible stories,
Badly spelled in rickety, limping letters,
"Help me—deaf, etc.—one of seven
        Brothers and sisters."

Others still accost the conspicuous lovers,
Plying flowers looted from cemeteries,
Buds already wilting, though filched from Tuesday's
        Sumptuous funeral.

Who's to say which one of them finally snags you,
One you will remember from all that pass you,
One that makes you fish through your cluttered pockets,
        Costing you something:

Maybe it's the girl with the funeral roses,
Five more left, her last, and you buy the whole lot,
Watching her run skipping away, work over,
      Into the darkness;

Maybe it's the boy with the flute he fashioned
Out of plastic straws, and his strident singing,
Snatches from a melody in a language
      No one can teach you.

V

# Explaining an Affinity for Bats

That they are only glimpsed in silhouette,
And seem something else at first—a swallow—
And move like new tunes, difficult to follow,
Staggering towards an obstacle they yet
Avoid in a last-minute pirouette,
Somehow telling solid things from hollow,
Sounding out how high a space, or shallow,
Revising into deepening violet.

That they sing—not the way the songbird sings
(Whose song is rote, to ornament, finesse)—
But travel by a sort of song that rings
True not in utterance, but harkenings,
Who find their way by calling into darkness
To hear their voice bounce off the shape of things.

# Variations on an Old Standard

Come let us kiss. This cannot last—
Too late is on its way too soon—
And we are going nowhere fast.

Already it is after noon,
That momentary palindrome.
The midday hours start to swoon—

Around the corner lurks the gloam.
The sun flies at half-mast, and flags.
The color guard of bees heads home,

Whizzing by in zigs and zags,
Weighed down by the dusty gold
They've hoarded in their saddlebags,

All the summer they can hold.
It is too late to be too shy:
The Present tenses, starts to scold—

Tomorrow has no alibi,
And hides its far side like the moon.
The bats inebriate the sky,

And now mosquitoes start to tune
Their tiny violins. I see,
Rising like a grey balloon,

The head that does not look at me,
And in its face, the shadow cast,
The Sea they call Tranquility—

Dry and desolate and vast,
Where all passions flow at last.
Come let us kiss. It's after noon,
And we are going nowhere fast.

# Bad News Blues

When Bad News comes to town, hold on to your heart.
When Bad News comes to town, the troubles start.
He's a hit, marked with a bullet, climbing the chart.

His smile swings open like a pocketknife.
He smiles like he could slice right through a life.
Nobody's daughter is safe. Nobody's wife.

He plays the odds. He needs just half a chance.
Sooner or later he'll ask *you* to dance.
He gets his own way like an ambulance.

He's got your number, and he dials direct.
He's calling you long distance and collect.
You gasp—something is wrong, somebody's wrecked.

He's standing outside your door. It's quarter to three.
You know he's out there, and it's quarter to three.
There is no knock. He's got the skeleton key.

# Two Rhymes for Grown-Ups

*1. Drinking Song*

The moon is chalky, white & thin.
The moon is bitter as aspirin.
She drinks it down with a glass of gin.

Clear and strong the moonbeams fall
As the proof of alcohol,
And everything they touch, appall.

But there are stars for all her ills—
A scattering of spilled, white pills.
The glass is sweating as it chills.

## 2. Hang-Up

The telephone is threatening suicide,
Weeping shrill
As a jilted bride,
Trilling, I will, I will.
When has it ever lied?

Its black umbilical slinks
Into the wall,
It's listening in. It thinks,
Nudging towards the brinks,
We never call.

It wails in its cradle, look,
What we forsook,
Angry as cancer.

And we will never be off the hook,
And there's no answer.

# Another Lullaby for Insomniacs

Sleep, she will not linger:
She turns her moon-cold shoulder.
With no ring on her finger,
You cannot hope to hold her.

She turns her moon-cold shoulder
And tosses off the cover.
You cannot hope to hold her:
She has another lover.

She tosses off the cover
And lays the darkness bare.
She has another lover,
Her heart is otherwhere.

She lays the darkness bare.
You slowly realize
Her heart is otherwhere.
There's distance in her eyes.

You slowly realize
That she will never linger,
With distance in her eyes
And no ring on her finger.

# Lullaby near the Railroad Tracks

Go back to sleep. The hour is small.
      A freight train between stations
Shook you out of sleep with all
      Its lonely ululations.

Through the stillness, while you slumber,
      They trundle down the track,
Lugging cattle, coal, and lumber,
      Crying, "alack, alack."

It's cheap to pay the engineer:
      The moon's a shiny dime.
Shut your eyes and you will hear
      The Doppler shift of time.

The hour is small. Resume your rest.
      Tomorrow will be kinder.
Here comes a freight train nosing west,
      Pulling the dawn behind her.

# On the Nearest Pass of Mars in
##    Sixty Thousand Years

War or Strife—yes, you were always painted
Incarnadine, hematic, flushed with passion,
Sanguine—we depicted you acquainted
With ruby hues the rage in mortal fashion.
And yet to see you ever closer, rolling
Elliptical through emptiness, our gazes
Are met now with a gaze past our controlling,
Red as an eyeball through which blood amazes,
And stony blind. Although we have created
Gods and goddesses of loathing, doting,
They neither love nor hate us, are defeated
By telescopes that taper into nothing,
A stare reflecting on itself, a pleasure
Cold and ferric, nothing we can treasure.

# XII Klassikal Lymnaeryx

*i*

Lady Circe declared, "Men are swine—
For when you invite them to dine,
        They smack while they eat.
        Plus, their small, cloven feet
Cannot open a bottle of wine."

*ii*

The poor fellow never suspects
That there's something all wrong with the sex—
        To affairs of that kind
        He has always been blind.
All he touches, that Oedipus wrecks.

*iii*

On a precipice stony and steep,
King Aegeus gazed on the deep.
        "If my son's sails are black,
        Then he ain't coming back!"
And he looked before taking a leap.

*iv*

Empedocles, addled with Drāno,
Declared, "I'm a god! What do *they* know?
      I'll *prove* I'm immortal!"
      And jumped through a portal—
The mouth of an active volcano.


*v*

With a great mind so tragically fertile,
Aeschylus won wreaths of myrtle.
      And yet his demise
      Could win Comic first prize—
To be brained by a hurtling turtle!


*vi*

Polyphemus, the Cyclops, would claim,
Hurling stones, his one eye was to blame
      For his failure to—*darn*—
      Hit the side of a barn,
Since he lacked depth perception to aim.

*vii*

Arachne, Athena beside her,
Let her ego grow wider and wider.
      "Let's see who's the winner—
      The very best spinner!"
Then she vanished, and nobody spied her.


*viii*

Cried Theseus, "I'm at a loss!
Perplexed by this puzzle, and cross!"
      "You can solve it! Don't whine,"
      Ariadne said, "twine
Does the trick. In a pinch, dental floss."


*ix*

Zeus knew that his wife would despise her,
Still he hoped that she'd be none the wiser.
      "Io, that cow!"
      Hera screamed. Zeus said, "How
Did you know? I thought it would disguise her."

*x*

Stoic Seneca wasn't a hero
To take on a pupil like Nero.
      But I tell you, in those days,
      It took some cojones
To give his assignments a zero.


*xi*

An atomist known as Lucretius,
Uttered, and wasn't facetious,
      "Death's nothing to dread.
      You can't feel once you're dead!"
But I still find the argument specious.


*xii*

*King Minos to Pasiphaë:*

"My trust in you's tacit yet full—
But dear, *what* are you trying to pull?
      A child should be cooing—
      Not lowing, or mooing—
You say this kid's mine? That's all bull!"

# Sisyphus

It is good to work
the dumb, obsessive
muscles. Exertion draws
the mind from hope
to a more tangible object.
To live

is to relive.
This can only work
when there is an object
to push, cursive and recursive,
up the hill, when you hope
this draws

to no close as day withdraws,
but will replay in dreams. You live
in hope
of dream-work,
its regressive,
infinite object.

Awake, abject,
the conscious mind draws
into a ball; the Elusive
tongues it like the pit of an olive.
The quirk
of hope

in recurrent nightmares is the hope
at last to be the object
of the murderer's handiwork,
when he draws
the knife to relieve
the stutter, to make passive

the massive
machinery of hope,
the broken record of alive.
Why object?
The luck of all the draws
is the weight of stone.

*Work*
*without hope draws nectar in a sieve*
*and hope without an object cannot live.*

# Song for the Women Poets

Sing, sing, because you can.
Descend in murk and pitch.
Double-talk the ferryman
And three-throated bitch.

Sing before the king and queen,
Make the grave to grieve,
Till Persephone weeps kerosene
And wipes it on her sleeve.

And she will grant you your one wish:
To fetch across a river
Black and sticky as licorice
The one you lost forever.

*Don't look back*. But no one heeds.
You glance down in the water.
The image drowning in the weeds
Could be your phantom daughter.

And part of you leaves Tartarus,
But part stays there to dwell—
You who are both Orpheus
And She he left in Hell.

 VI

# Jet Lag

Oriented, suddenly Aurora,
I rise without alarm in the random dark,
Already full of purpose, without coffee
Or tea, to the cat's delight, revving her pleasure.

Breakfast is a poem, light, in good measure,
A grapefruit split to reveal the spokes and rays
Of the sunburst wheels on a golden chariot.
I dress, I shake the dewdrops from tips of my tresses.

It is as if I can hear them, imagined horses,
Astir in the stable, fogging the air with their breath,
Snug under blankets, awaiting the curry comb
And oats, ready to set out over the hill,

Over the sleeping city, over the sill
Of the sea, islands dribbled like pancake batter,
Knowing where I am is always East,
Always ahead of the day that's going to matter.

# Clean Monday

*for Anastasi*

Other kites already patched the sky,
As if the clouds were moored with so much string.
To fly a kite seemed like an easy thing.
We fastened on the tail, perhaps awry.

Your nephew gave our offering to the breeze.
It lurched aloft, wagged side to side, and stooped,
And, in an angry handwriting, it looped
Until it suicided in the trees.

An hour to retrieve and fix the craft.
Your nephew strayed away to other games.
We untied knots, and called each other names,
And realized our pettiness, and laughed.

We wrestled with the angel of the air
Until we got his blessing, and the kite
Reared up against the string with all its might,
And your nephew sprinted back to clap and stare.

Then, "Let me hold it please!" he wheedled me.
"But with both hands," I said. And he, "I will."
For a moment he was sailing standing still,
Then in his joy, forgot, and set it free.

# The Song Rehearsal

*Degas, National Gallery of Scotland*

It seems familiar somehow, though it's set
In a parlor in New Orleans—another age.
It's summer—the furniture is draped in white.
A shadowed man looks up from the piano.
Two women are rehearsing a duet—
One is striding down an imagined stage
In full-throated aria, the other,
Turning her face away, holds up her right
Hand against the blast of shrill soprano.

But reading the little plaque, I understand—
The casual scene from life begins to change
To genre. The woman with the lifted hand,
Turning away, as if half-terrified,
With loose, high-waisted skirt, will be a mother.
The singer bearing down on her, mouth wide,
Is the angel trumpeting the news so strange,
So ordinary, it's difficult to believe—
And greater than anything she could conceive.

# Prelude

Lately, at the beginning of concerts when
The first-chair violin
Plays the A four-forty and the bows
Go whirring about the instruments like wings
Over unfingered strings,
The cycling fifths, spectral arpeggios,

As the oboe lights the pure torch of the note,
Something in my throat
Constricts and tears are startled to my eyes
Helplessly. And lately when I stand
Torn ticket in my hand
In the foyers of museums I surprise

You with a quaver in my rote reply—
Again I overbrim
And corners of the room go prismed, dim.
You'd like to think that it is Truth and Art
That I am shaken by,
So that I must discharge a freighted heart;

But it is not when cellos shoulder the tune,
Nor changing of the key
Nor resolution of disharmony
That makes me almost tremble, and it is not
The ambered afternoon
Slanting through motes of dust a painter caught

Four hundred years ago as someone stands
Opening the blank
Future like a letter in her hands.
It is not masterpieces of first rank,
Not something made
By once-warm fingers, nothing painted, played.

No, no. It is something else. It is something raw
That suddenly falls
Upon me at the start, like loss or awe—
The vertigo of possibility—
The pictures I don't see,
The open strings, the perfect intervals.

# Ultrasound

What butterfly—
Brain, soul, or both—
Unfurls here, pallid
As a moth?

(Listen, here's
Another ticker,
Counting under
Mine, and quicker.)

In this cave
What flickers fall,
Adumbrated
On the wall?—

Spine like beads
Strung on a wire,
Abacus
Of our desire,

Moon-face where
Two shadows rhyme,
Two moving hands
That tell the time.

I am the room
The future owns,
The darkness where
It grows its bones.

**Visiting the Grave of Rupert Brooke**

It was on Skyros, in the middle of the Aegean, that Rupert Brooke was buried in 1915, having died of blood poisoning on his way to Gallipoli.

**The Modern Greek for "Nightmare" Is *Ephialtes***

Ephialtes was the Greek who betrayed the Spartans to the Persians at Thermopylae; it is also the name of the ancient demon of nightmare.

**Clean Monday**

Clean Monday marks the first day of Greek Orthodox Lent. Children celebrate it by flying kites.

**On the Nearest Pass of Mars in Sixty Thousand Years**

This poem was commissioned for an anthology of sonnets using the rhyme words of Shakespeare's Sonnet 20.

**Sisyphus**

"Work without Hope draws nectar in a sieve / And Hope without an object cannot live" is from Coleridge's sonnet "Work Without Hope."

A C K N O W L E D G M E N T S

My thanks to the editors of the following magazines, in which these poems first appeared: *Able Muse* ("To Speke of Wo That Is in Mariage," "Cassandra"); *The Atlantic Monthly* ("Amateur Iconography: Resurrection"); *Beloit Poetry Journal* and *The Best American Poetry 2000* ("Asphodel"); *Blackbird* ("Noir"); *The Classical Outlook* ("XII Klassikal Lymnaeryx"); *The Cortland Review* ("Athens, August"); *Evansville Review* ("Antiblurb"); *Five Points* ("Clean Monday"); *The Formalist* ("Explaining an Affinity for Bats," "Jet Lag," "Visiting the Grave of Rupert Brooke," "Bad News Blues"); *The Hudson Review* ("An Ancient Dog Grave, Unearthed During Construction of the Athens Metro"); *Iambs & Trochees* ("Lovejoy Street," "Empty Icon Frame"); *Iron Horse Literary Review* ("Flying Colors: Flags of Convenience") *Leviathan Quarterly* ("Minutes"); *Light* ("Lullaby near the Railroad Tracks"); *Link* ("*Ubi Sunt* Lament for the Eccentric Museums of My Childhood"); *The National Poetry Review* ("Nettles"); *The Nebraska Review* ("Last Will," "On the Nearest Pass of Mars in Sixty Thousand Years"); *The New Criterion* ("Mornings, I Walk Past the First Cemetery of Athens," "Variations on an Old Standard"); *Oxford American* ("The Village in the Lake"); *Pivot* ("Song for the Women Poets"); *Poetry* ("Dead Language Lesson," "Failure," "The Modern Greek for 'Nightmare' Is *Ephialtes*," "The Dollhouse," "Implements from the 'Tomb of the Poet,'" "Apotropaic," "Arrowhead Hunting," "Sine Qua Non," "Evil Eye," "Drinking Song," "Actaeon," "Another Lullaby for Insomniacs," "Sisyphus," "Prelude," "Hang-Up," "The Song Rehearsal"); *The Sewanee Theological Review* ("The Charioteer"); *Shenandoah* ("Thyme"); *32 Poems* ("Clean Break," "Ultrasound");

*Washington Square* ("Alice, Grown-up, at the Cocktail Party"); *The Yale Review* ("Aftershocks," "Fragment").

Several of the poems in this volume appeared in a limited-edition letterpress chapbook, *Aftershocks,* printed by Michael Peich at the Aralia Press.

Special thanks to the Hawthornden Castle International Retreat for Writers (and my fellow inmates) for a month of peace in decent ease, during which some of these poems were written, and many others revised or conceived.

Definitions of *hapax* are taken from Liddell and Scott's *Greek-English Lexicon* and *Webster's Third New International Dictionary*.

A. E. Stallings was born in 1968 and grew up in Decatur, Georgia. She has received numerous awards for her poetry, including the Richard Wilbur Award, the 2004 Frederick Bock Prize, a Pushcart Prize, and the Howard Nemerov Sonnet Award. Stallings studied classics in Athens, Georgia, and now lives in Athens, Greece. She is married to the journalist John Psaropoulos, and they have a son, Jason.